WRITE from
the HEART

Amused Musings to Advance Your Craft

WRITE from

the HEART

Amused Musings to Advance Your Craft

Printed in the United States of America
Published by Quintessence   First Printing August 2017

Jeffrey J.Michaels.com
Cover Image – Romolo Tavani/Shutterstock
ISBN # 978-0-9969371-4-6

"DREAM BIG
AND DARE TO FAIL"

~ Norman Vaughan

PREFACE

SO YOU WANNABE A WRITER? Big name author with limo and multi-million-dollar contract in hand? Or quiet contemplative who is penning the great American...no! The great GLOBAL novel. The one that inspires everyone to get along and unite so that when the cosmic entities return, be they angel or alien, they will first seek you out to give you that special chair of honor?

The book you hold in your hands is going to help you get a grip on your dreams, wealth or wisdom, either one. By "get a grip" I mean explain the reality of the writing world and your place within that strange society.

This is not an instruction book. There are plenty of those. They are all good in some way and different in their approach despite saying the same essential things over and over again. Those are brain books. They are about structure and The Rules. By all means buy a couple and learn your craft. Read those last three words again: Learn Your Craft.

But this book, the slim tome you are holding gingerly, wondering whether it is worth your hard-earned dollars or, more importantly, your valuable time, this book will help you navigate the emotional state of being a writer. Here I will try to inspire you and en*courage* you. That root word, courage, comes from the old Latin (maybe Greek or possibly French - I am no scholar), meaning "from the heart" and it is here that the best creative results begin. I will also try to entertain and amuse you. Perhaps even coax a laugh.

At the same time I will not pull any punches regarding the reality of what you will face in following the path of writer to author, from scribbler of notes to published and printed. One of the most vital truths I can tell you is this:

There are more people making money on writers than there are writers making money on writing.

Now, if after reading and absorbing that fact, you are still willing to take the emotional risk, still feeling the pull of creativity, still hearing the call of the Path of the Storyteller, then read on! Laugh at my attempts at humor, endure my stretched similes and mangled metaphors, thrill to my literary craft, and face palm at my convoluted sentence structure.

But above all, take courage. Take heart. Write, and write the best story you can. Above all, enjoy yourself. Why do anything if it does not bring you and others joy?

INTRODUCTION

TEACHING WRITERS

I WAS A POOR STUDENT. I was inattentive and distracted. I did not see the point in much of what was being taught. This does not mean I was not an excellent student in my own self-directed studies. It just means my concern for grades and high marks was never a priority and the report card displayed my errant scholastic attention. My "permanent record" during matriculation is likely abysmal. I am unsure of the truth of that last statement because I am unsure of where exactly my permanent record is being stored. Also, I don't care.

I suspect many creatives have a similar lament when it comes to their own school experience. We probably looked the same as one another, nose in a book (non-required and possibly forbidden), scribbling in notebooks (weird thoughts and observations about Those Others), volumes of stories and poems that were unassigned and unappreciated by the legions of grammarians who existed to inflict the proper use of sentence diagrams and enforce punctuation marks and bring to abrupt halt anything that might look like a run-on sentence, rather than assist in crafting artistically creative communications.

Ah yes! Grammar: that "set of structural rules governing the composition of clauses, phrases, and words in any given natural language. The term refers also to the study of such rules, and this field includes phonology, morphology, and syntax, often complemented by phonetics, semantics, and pragmatics," as that great scholarly democratizer Wikipedia puts it.

As writers we do not often sit down and write a story by first thinking, "How will I utilize the syntax of each sentence to clearly express the morphology of each character's meaning in the dialogue to enhance the allegory and symbolism of my epic retelling of Moby Dick?" Well maybe some of us do, but personally I just sit down and start to write a tale or an article that interests me and hopefully will capture an audience's attention. I never ever diagram a sentence.

The rules, as they are, can be interesting, but the creative spirit is not often fed by structure. Most of us learn storytelling by reading and watching stories. Everything from Citizen Kane to Bewitched, from Gilgamesh to the Twilight series, informs us of styles and substance, or lack thereof. We may not even understand that we are learning the craft, but subconsciously we engage mentally and emotionally with the words and images and the order, the structure, in which they are presented. When we sit down to tell our own tale it often will sound similar to the type of story we personally enjoy.

As children, our first (likely wretched) efforts at communicating a story further instruct us. In all probability we receive enthusiastic but, as we age, fading criticism from busy mom and dad. What is a literary or artistic triumph to a five year old is not deemed worthy when we turn fifteen. Besides, the refrigerator door is reserved for primal, Crayola explorations, not double-spaced typed themes of five hundred words on what it means to be a good citizen or why Melville is important to the modern age.

Our early creations are generally some permutation of existing narratives shared at bedtime (books our parents recall from their childhood) or in Storytime at the local library (books deemed worthy by a committee and included in a list published in a peer reviewed journal). These youthful inventions are an amalgamation of fairy tales and television commercials processed deep in our tiny minds and regurgitated out of our energetic little guts in an effort to make sense out of our world. This process changes little as we get older, by the way. It is only that we become more sophisticated in our skill set. And also in what we feed our brains upon.

We learn lessons in the telling of the tale, or "showing" if you are following popular trends in writing instruction. Note: I am not. And neither are a lot of other authors, though we give lip service to the maxim. Please don't tell them I told you.

Life experience is often more important in creative endeavor than formal training. This is not meant to say that formal training is useless. Far from it. Only, if you learn what has been done before and have those lessons reinforced as The Absolute, Entirely Correct, This-Is-What-the-Manual-Says way you will likely write to please the past.

It might be heresy to say that Charles Dickens, if writing to a modern-day audience, is in need of an editor, so I won't say that. I will say that styles shift and change. No one in the late nineteenth or early twentieth centuries would conceive of such a thing as flash fiction and any attempt would quickly have been relegated to the category of poetry and forced into a rhyming cadence. Limericks are the original flash fiction. These days the internet has altered our perceptions of storytelling beyond the craziest of ideas imagined by Lord Dunsany or H.P. Lovecraft. And they of course learned from those who went before. But they did not duplicate.

If you get a crazy idea and don't know any better, you might, in your blissful ignorance, just try something that has not been attempted before. Children do this. They sit down and just draw and they do not naturally insist that all trees be green, or all fish remain in the water. The raw, unfiltered stories I see from newbie writers, the so-called uneducated, are frequently full of errors, true, but fueled with high concepts and fresh approach. Once that pure creative expression exists, it can always be shaped into a Grade A, First Class book. And we do that by *then* applying the lessons that matter, therefore not dampening the creative spirit.

School. Hide bound it may be, but the rules are there for a reason, much like traffic signs. Still, the road less taken leads places not often seen. It can be lonely to be the rule breaker, the weird kid on the bus, and it may never lead to great success monetarily, but the critics tend to trash the tropes and formula of those who learned to write by the book. As it were.

It is said that we should write the story we ourselves desire to read. Do you really want to read the same story someone else wrote? If that is the case, why write? Your assignment for Monday is five hundred words on why you want to be a writer.

Table of Contents

1

I'D LIKE TO START PROCRASTINATING,

BUT I JUST CAN'T FIND THE TIME

THE FOLLOWING IS BASED ON A SEMI-TRUE STORY that happened to, um, a friend of mine, a guy I know. Not me. It is pieced together from his notes and internal dialogue, also known as omniscient narrating. Perhaps a bit of unreliable narrating as well.

Here are his words: "It is said that we teach that which we must learn. Today's topic will be the setting of goals. I so suck at that goal-setting stuff. In fact, this article was started last year! And here it is 1999! Well at least I am getting around to finishing it before the 21st Century gets into full swing. It will take that long to get edited by the staff at Writers 'R' Us

Magazine, sent to the presses, folded, stitched, and shipped to all the many brick and mortar bookstores where hopeful authors hang out and drink coffee while taking notes on their legal pads so that when they get home they can transfer their literary genius into the miracle electronic box called a computer. Thank the ghost of Gutenberg for Windows 98! I myself have plenty of handwritten notes for this article that I just have to type into the machine. So I'll be right back! Right after I check my electronic mail account…Hmmm…what is this internet thing?

"2005 – Okay. Setting goals means keeping track of your progress by writing down the date you start and then making a firm, solid deadline. I'll figure out my end date later. This time I really have a handle on the topic. I have been studying and making notes and listening to motivational speakers for years. And here is what I have learned. If you want to get anything done you need to set some goals. An idea without a goal is simply a wish. Or wishful thinking. Something like that. Let me check my quote. Gosh I love Google! Be right back.

"2011 – I'd forgotten about this article! I wonder if the magazine is still interested in my proposal. I wonder if the magazine is still being published. I guess it would work as a blog post. Okay, here is the quote I wanted to use: 'A goal isn't automatically a goal. It is a dream until you write it down. Then it is a goal. Or a book.' Hmmm…that ain't quite right. Maybe it's, 'A goal without a plan is just a wish.' Wait a sec, let me do a search online for the correct quote…Hey, this website about writing looks interesting.

"2014 – Wow! There is a LOT of truth to this goal-setting stuff. But OMG! Pantsers will never quite get the structure part of goal setting. That is a problem in writing a blog on goal setting. Pantsers will just want to wait for inspiration. How can I address this part? I think I will meditate and wait for my Muse to show up…

"2016 – The Age of Internetlightenment – At last I can see the value of waiting for my Muse while actually showing up at the keyboard, which is where my Muse expects to find me! At last I comprehend that if I am truly a professional writer I must behave the same way I would if I were a professional anything else!"

NECESSARY SELF-DISCIPLINE

There is a lot of potential leeway available to the professional writer, but there is also necessary self-discipline that is more important. Here are some guidelines I personally find useful. Adapt them to your own style and energy. Vibe yourself to the basic notes and jazz, baby, jazz!

Write down your PRIMARY GOAL. If this is not something you can immediately identify, then all the other steps will be purposeless. This need not be very specific. Your primary goal as a writer should be to become published, with the best possible product you can create and craft. The way to accomplish this is to understand that "Finished" and "Perfect" do not easily exist together. Goals will help you finish. The more you finish, the more perfect you will become.

CHOICES YOU MUST MAKE ONLY ONE TIME

Choose a fixed workspace and create a specific time to start. Couple this with a time to finish. Note: You can enjoy flextime for your professional writer business, but remember you are trying to set some energetic structure to assist in creating not just stories but FINISHED STORIES!

Choose a planned number of pages to complete each day. (See Ajay Ohri's Guidelines for Writers below.)

Create a simple ritual that signals it is starting time. I find it helpful to light a fire, a candle, or stick of incense, for example, but it can be as simple as taking a deep breath or putting on headphones.

GOALS TO ACCOMPLISH DAILY

Review yesterday's work but DO NOT EDIT. Begin by beginning. Just start where you left off and type until you gain momentum. You can always cut the unworthy words. Conclude when you have all the words necessary for the day, but make sure you have achieved your word count. Write more, but not less.

If you must, build in a SMALL AMOUNT OF TIME on social media. SET A TIMER! While online, focus on your business and writing contacts when in your work space/time. Platform is useless if you have no product.

GOALS TO ACCOMPLISH WEEKLY

Review the work you did this week (Do NOT Judge!). Determine any narrative or structural problems that need to be addressed. Make a list, check it twice, try to find any pages that are naughty and/or nice. If you are writing a naughty book, then you can keep some of the former pages.

Take ONE DAY and do some first draft editing. Break apart overlong paragraphs. Spell check sections of the manuscript. Do a light punctuation scan. Do not get bogged down in details at this point. This is just a little light housekeeping to gain perspective on the story as a whole.

Goals to accomplish MONTHLY

Based on your weekly review process, determine if you need to revise your outline.

It is easy to become isolated and lose perspective on your project(s). A monthly critique group can help. Can't find one? Start one! A note of caution: This can be a daunting task. Especially for creatives who lack organizational drive and are likely to be introverted to some degree. Critiques groups MUST be heavily structured and there MUST be someone willing to exercise iron control over everyone else's ego. And that person need also be kind and gentle. Like a border Collie herding kittens. Feisty, fierce kittens.

Finding a group that you fit in can be equally daunting. Don't be afraid to join and don't be afraid to quit a group. Only, do not quit just because someone gives you a critique that you do not like. That is what they are there for.

Each month, ask yourself: "Have I nourished my Muse? Have I done anything to increase my craft and skills?" These are things that can be done outside the normal working hours. Go see a movie, watch a series of TV shows, read a book or three. AND while you are doing this pay attention to what works for you and what leaves you thinking, "I can write better than that!" Now when you sit down at your work space remember what you said and DO IT!

REALITY CHECK

The following is a helpful list of realities compiled by Ajay Ohri. Regarding the numbers, don't be dogmatic. They are approximations, not rules.

- Write 50 words. That is a paragraph.
- Write 400 words. That is a page.
- Write 300 pages. That is a manuscript.
- Write every day. That is a habit.
- Edit and Rewrite. That is how you get better.
- Spread your writing for people to comment. That is called feedback.
- Don't worry about rejection or publication. That's a writer.
- When not writing, read. Read from writers better than you. Read and perceive.

Describing yourself as a writer indicates you are writing. When you are not writing, you are not a writer. You are a sitter. You are an internetter. You are a Facebooker, a movie-er, a TVer. Dreaming is creative, but without placing words in a document that can be seen by others, dreaming and procrastination look a lot alike.

Writing is a verb. Action, active, act. Writer, write!

"Write while the heat is in you. The writer who postpones the recording of his thoughts uses an iron which has cooled to burn a hole with."

 ~ Henry David Thoreau

"When I'm writing, I write. And then it's as if the muse is convinced that I'm serious and says, 'Okay. Okay. I'll come." ~ Maya Angelou

2

PANTSERS BECOME PLOTTERS: A LOVE STORY

"WHO," as the caterpillar asked Alice, "are YOU?"

It is an apt question that we as writers often ask our characters. Sometimes we ask before the book begins to be written and sometimes we just write and learn who they are as we go along. What you do in this regard defines who YOU are as an author.

I am referring to the archetypes labeled "Pantsers" and "Plotters" and presenting primary differences betwixt the two. Perhaps we can discover something about ourselves as aspiring authors and move to the middle ground, where most of the action happens.

PANTSERS

Pantsers are so called because they write their stories "by the seat of their pants," which is an old aeronautical term essentially defined as doing something complicated without sufficient experience or ability. In other words, Pantsers have no idea what is coming next in their story, for it comes out of thin air, delivered pristine to the page by the elusive Muse. The Pantsers are mere scribes. And proud of it.

PLOTTERS

Plotters are called such because they are deeply organized prior to beginning a book or story project. They possess vast files of three by five cards (or the digital equivalent) delineating each character's biography from conception to the moment they are introduced in the narrative, as well as a minute-by-minute timeline of the days, months, or years in which the action of their tale takes place.

CHAOS VERSUS CONTROL

Pantsers are agents of chaos. Plotters are control freaks. Pantsers are befriended by their Muse and await inspiration. Plotters are inspired every day at the same time when they sit down to work.

Pantsers are eloquent and poetic, weaving spells with their verbiage and inspired phraseology. Their writing possesses a transcendent beauty that translates the sizzling of bacon and the steam from a whistling tea kettle into the perfect emotional simile of crisp early autumn in a forgotten village in Vermont. Near a pristine lakeside, the morning mist rises and blurs the demarcation between the pond and the shore. The dew, heavy and deep, soaks all things equally, granting moist nourishment, sans judgment.

Plotters have a three-book contract with an advance and two more novels in the pipeline. It's a series about a divorced sheriff living in rural Vermont where bodies float up from local lake on a semi-regular basis. He must solve the mystery while helping his young, precocious daughter cope with the old-fashioned school marm, who is soon replaced (due to the inciting incident in Chapter Two) by the hip young red-head with green eyes, hailing from Manhattan, who recently graduated with a Masters in Special Education and Ancient Akkadian Cuneiform Writing. She takes the job teaching in a small rural school for mysterious reasons not revealed until Book Three of the series, when she and the rural sheriff (who once worked on the Chicago SWAT unit) consummate their romantic tension with a dramatic kiss as they believe they are about to perish at the hands of the diabolical logging company executive. HBO and Starz are bidding for the rights.

ARTISTRY

When confronted by an editor who wants the Pantser to tighten up the manuscript's prose and make it more like Hemingway, the Pantser will recoil in Faulknerian agony, decrying the editor as a barbarian. He will then indignantly adjust his beret, scoop up his treasured prose and say, "It is experimental! How dare you seek to make such hallowed dialogue COMMON!" and sweep out of the room. (Or, at the very least, hit the send button with sharp indignation.)

To recover from the humiliation of having to deal with such an artistic infidel, the Pantser will retire to his local favorite Muse-summoning space, a dark bar that offers free baskets of peanuts and you throw the empty shells on the wooden floor, or an independent coffeehouse with an interior so dark the black-clad baristas appear and disappear like caffeinated ninjas after taking your order for the darkest roasts available to man (with room), or an off-the-beaten-path restaurant down a side alley where they serve thick soups in bread bowls and offer extra bread, hard and crusty, and dining is al fresco.

There, the Pantser will fume for a time and, in a show of disdain for societal convention, will, with stylistic flare, light up a Gauloises, casting defiant glances at any who dare frown at the thick, Turkish smoke that emanates from his artistic nostrils. The only other patron will be smoking a Gitanes. Their eyes will meet, and narrow. They will nod silently, knowingly, at one another. They will never see each other again but will become a character in the other's book about the new lost generation.

OVER-ACHIEVER

Elsewhere, the Plotter will embrace every change requested by that same editor. She will not only tighten the words and paragraphs, but also recognize that some of the excised material can be recycled into her new concept of a space-faring marshal who is raising a precocious daughter after his wife departs on a generational starship to colonize a distant planet, leaving him to patrol a backwater section of the solar system, which is boring until the arrival of a green-eyed red-haired teacher, no, FIGHTER PILOT! Well, the details can be worked out, but this has multi-book contract written all over it!

And with that shallow insight, the Plotter will feel that she has become inspired by her Muse, because the Plotter's goals for writing are different than the Pantser's.

COMMON GROUND

But one day, the Pantser notes that he is stuck in a dead- end job as a manager of a local indie bookstore that is in a perpetual state of going out of business, because ...Amazon! He will find himself in a late-night session of a Rogue Read and Critique at his favorite writers conference, where he will overhear the Plotter bemoaning the sameness of her own writing. She wishes she could break free of the tyranny of repetitive genre work and write something worthy. Something like the Pantser's Literary Romantic Coming of Age Autumnal Vermont Near Pond novel that was published by a small independent press and is doing moderately well on the Amazon bestseller lists.

Later, in the hotel bar, they will sit near each other, privately contemplating their moderately middle-aged literary lives. The Pantser will nurse a Guinness or whatever dark-ish stout-like beer he can attain from the limited hotel stock. The Plotter, thinking about writing a Noir novel, will sip a nondescript red wine, (not quite the color of her dark ruby lipstick that now smears the lip of the once clean wine glass like blood from a cut lip). The house red is a vaguely unfulfilling replacement of the Plotter's favorite Pinot Noir, acceptable solely because the young woman tending bar has never heard of Pinot anything and failed to grasp the clever reference to the late night atmosphere and the term Noir. The Pantser will laugh wryly at the Plotter's jest and their eyes will meet in the mirror.

The Pantser and the Plotter will hit it off, having similar writing issues, though coming at them from two extreme points. Over the coming years, they will strike emotional bargains with each other and argue their causes to and fro, eventually coming to mutual respect for one another's achievements. They will read and critique each other's work, and they will purposely attend conferences and book launches and library events for local published authors. They will offer one another emotional support. Separately, they will continue to eke out a living until, one evening when the conference hotel has screwed up their reservations forcing them to share a room, they will fall in love. *Whoa! I did not see THAT coming!*

TOGETHER, WE ARE BETTER

Soon, the Plotter will find she is writing expressively and more from her heart. She will uncover that elusive sense of fulfillment that her red-haired green-eyed love interests perpetually sought in the laconic, strong, gruff, but fair-minded protagonists who helmed all her mysterious romances, her adventurous romances, or her romantic science fictional space operas.

Meanwhile, the Pantser has let his artistic guard down enough to trust what the Plotter recommends and, realizing that she is not his enemy for counseling some streamlining of text, will discover that plotting the second act actually strengthens his story and allows him to make an understandable point to his tale. People will appreciate his subtle use of structure while still enjoying his prose and clever words. With her assistance, he will avoid the sophomore slump and actually gain praise for his second book, as well as the interest of an agent for his next work of high-concept literate art. He does not yet confide that he's got nothing more to say.

Secretly, the Pantser and the Plotter will be writing together under a pseudonym, making a decent living churning out erotic romances that take place in the Old West, in Epic Viking days, in Merry Olde England, in Chivalrous France, and Renaissance Italy. They will travel the world together doing research and writing off the expenses on their taxes.

In time, a child will be born, and they will have high hopes for their literate little one. She will grow up to be a mathematician.

In the end, the Pantser and the Plotter, like the King and the Pawn, will go into the same box after the game is complete.

"The most beautiful things are those that madness prompts and reason writes." ~ Andre Gide

"There are three points of view from which a writer can be considered: he may be considered as a storyteller, as a teacher, and as an enchanter. A major writer combines these three — storyteller, teacher, enchanter — but it is the enchanter in him that predominates and makes him a major writer."
 ~ Vladimir Nabokov

3

Searching for Greener Pastures

It is spring and, after a long cold lonely winter of starving in the attic gable apartment in Paris, many a young, creative human's fancy turns to thoughts of growth and gaining a market share. These days, there are so many paths to promotion.

An astonishing variety of people, groups, contests, magazines, books, and conferences will tell YOU the secrets to making BIG Money, that Greenback Dollar. Buy their product and you will see the vistas and sweet verdant valleys of success. All you need do is pay THEM a fee and you are guaranteed Bongo Bucks of the Great Googly

Moolah. (Wait…did they actually guarantee that? Read the fine print, tadpole.)

Here is the one secret that so many books on the art of writing fail to mention:

THERE ARE MORE PEOPLE MAKING MONEY ON WRITERS THAN THERE ARE WRITERS MAKING MONEY ON WRITING.

There, I have said it and now you know.

This is a hard lesson. One that will likely make new writers a bit uneasy. It is not something taught at writing schools. This is not to say that as an author you are doomed to a life of the pauper. It is only to point out that there is not an easy way to become the prince.

In fact, if you do achieve a measure of success (Agent, Publisher, Contract, New York Times Bestseller list) and you take all the money you make and divide it by the time you spent to gain said greenback dollars, you may find that you are actually earning less than minimum wage.

So why do it? Why write if there is little chance of monetary reward? There are other easier ways to make money. If you are a creative individual by nature, an artist, you already know the answer in your heart.

You might as well ask a seed why it germinates, why it opens and sprouts, why it creates a flower, plant, or tree against all the odds of shallow, barren soil, drought, being eaten by a bird, or failure to take root.

IT DOES IT BECAUSE IT IS A SEED.

That is what seeds do. They take the chance and sometimes they fail, but often they produce and succeed. Maybe not wildly, maybe they do not become a giant sequoia or abundant apple tree, but that is not what most seeds are for. Most create a plant that then creates a seed that looks much like the last one. This perpetuates the species and brings some small nourishment and enrichment of the air or soil where it dwells.

Sometimes we, humanity, gain because the seed produces a pleasurable fruit or vegetable or herb. Sometimes there is a pretty flower to be smelled and enjoyed.

More often than not the seed falls where there is no human to enjoy the fruits. Is that seed then useless? No. The birds, the bees, the soil itself, all these things are part of a vast cycle of life and death, dormancy and vitality.

SEEDS SPROUT.
WRITERS WRITE.

Writing is a form of therapy; sometimes I wonder how all those who do not write, compose or paint can manage to escape the madness, melancholia, the panic and fear which is inherent in a human situation. ~ Graham Greene

We tell stories to ourselves first, but maybe, if we fall on the correct type of soil and find enough sunlight and rainwater to nourish us, we create a pleasant story or nourishing parable that allows others to see their lives or the history of the human race in a different way.

Will our stories shake the world or reshape the path of civilization? Likely not, but we may create a line of writers who will. Our work may be light and temporary, a flower in the field, but the seeds we produce have meaning by their length of existence and their power of perpetuating ideas.

And sometimes…great crops grow; vast fields come about from many seeds sprouting together. Millions are fed; millions enjoy the beauty of flowers. Life is better and we can continue facing the challenges of global society.

AND SO YOU WRITE.
SOMETIMES THE REWARD IS THE ACT ITSELF.

But sometimes you show your work, and another human says, "This is great stuff!"

You feel that moment of personal growth, that instant where you sprout and break the soil into the light. You are exposed now. It is dangerous, but there is no going back!

You feel the roots strengthen and help stabilize you as your manuscript is seen by two, then four, then ten, and sometimes one hundred humans who read your work and all say, "This is a great book! This is exactly how I feel but could never explain it to anyone."

Hopefully, they tell their friends and your words and thoughts organically blossom, taking on a life of their own, and people respond to the book in ways they could not anticipate when it was a mere concept or outline.

Like the seed, you have risked all and now there is nothing to do but nurture the full-grown organism. Harvest some of the seeds from that same life form and prepare to plant once again. For that is why the seed creates a flower – to gain new seed.

And that is why you and I write, because it is what we do to propel the world into a continued existence of growth and beauty.

THE UNIVERSE IS A VAST CREATIVE ENERGY.
YOU ARE A PARTICLE OF THAT UNIVERSE.

You are an aspect of the creative power that forms all the diversity that we call existence.

When you write, you create, and in that action you align yourself with cosmic powers. It does not matter what you write: romance, suspense, mystery, or humor. Great literature and philosophy may have a claim on being more intellectually worthy, but we need all manner of plants and animals within the ecosystem.

LOWLY GRASSES AND INSECTS
HAVE AN EQUAL CONTRIBUTION TO LIFE
AS DO ORCHIDS AND SCIENTIFIC GENIUSES.

Maybe you are the untapped potential, the next big thing and, toiling away in a coffee shop or the tiny walk-in closet you have converted into a makeshift office, you cannot see your personal brilliance.

What if you finish your book? What if you take it to a conference? What if you show it to editors, agents, or critique groups that run late into the night? What if they actually LIKE your efforts and encourage you to seek publication? What if you become known as a great creative energy yourself? And what if you are the one in a million who hits the right chord with society and becomes the next big thing?

What if your project gets the green light? That is another story, and it is called, "The Grass is not Always Greener on the Other Side of the Hill of Success." The pressure will be on and there will be no time to be feeling green about the gills!

Of course if you do hit the big time and find yourself deep in folding green, I will be green with envy.

"I have been successful probably because I have always realized that I knew nothing about writing and have merely tried to tell an interesting story entertainingly." ~ Edgar Rice Burroughs

"There are three rules for writing the novel. Unfortunately, no one knows what they are."
~ William Somerset Maugham

4
CRAFTING MEMORABLE OPENING LINES

LET US TALK OF OPENING LINES. Where to start…

Every writer's conference and instructional course will emphasize the import, the absolutely vital, pivotal necessity of the first five words, the first five sentences, the first five paragraphs, and the first five pages as being paramount to selling your story. There is truth to this concept.

In the course of famous first lines the perennial fav tends to be, "In the Beginning God created the heavens and the earth." As an opening it certainly has scope and a fair amount of poetic supremacy. It may even be the best first line ever written. But (he said semi-blasphemously), it is not the only good one out there.

"An opening line should invite the reader to begin the story. It should say: Listen. Come in here. You want to know about this." ~ Stephen King, *On Writing.*

As such, *A Tale of Two Cities* holds a good place in literary history. You know the first part. It is such an ubiquitous part of our society, I bet you are saying it in your mind right now. But few know the full quote. It is really pretty awesome.

Charles Dickens writes, *"It was the best of times, it was the worst of times, it was the age of wisdom, it was the age of foolishness, it was the epoch of belief, it was the epoch of incredulity, it was the season of Light, it was the season of Darkness, it was the spring of hope, it was the winter of despair, we had everything before us, we had nothing before us, we were all going direct to Heaven, we were all going direct the other way… − in short, the period was so far like the present period, that some of its noisiest authorities insisted on its being received, for good or for evil, in the superlative degree of comparison only."*

Offhand I am not really sure who is speaking, but who cares!

My personal favorite is from a book everyone thinks they know, but most are wrong. Edgar Rice Burroughs' *Tarzan of the Apes* is a stunning tale of raw passion, an argument about nature vs. nurture, civilization vs. primal jungle law, inherent nobility vs. inherited noble titles. All of those high-concept philosophical elements, plus it has a great cold opening.

Here is an abbreviated version, but honestly, do yourself a favor and read the first book in the series. You will not regret it. *"I had this story from one who had no business to tell it to me, or to any other. I may credit the seductive influence of an old vintage upon the narrator for the beginning of it, and my own skeptical incredulity during the days that followed for the balance of the strange tale....I do not say the story is true, for I did not witness the happenings which it portrays, but the fact that in the telling of it to you I have taken fictitious names for the principal characters quite sufficiently evidences the sincerity of my own belief that it MAY be true."*

IT WAS A DARK AND STORMY NIGHT

Some first lines are memorable because they have been judged to be awful. "It was a dark and stormy night" is an often mocked and parodied phrase written by English novelist Edward Bulwer-Lytton in the opening sentence of his 1830 novel, *Paul Clifford*. But when you read the entire sentence, you may get a different view.

"It was a dark and stormy night; the rain fell in torrents — except at occasional intervals, when it was checked by a

violent gust of wind which swept up the streets (for it is in London that our scene lies), rattling along the housetops, and fiercely agitating the scanty flame of the lamps that struggled against the darkness."

Writer's Digest described this sentence as "the literary poster child for bad story starters." On the other hand, the American Book Review ranked it as No. 22 on its "Best First Lines from Novels list." What do you think?

What about your work? Do you have a good opening?

Are you spending time crafting the first five lines as carefully as Noah Lukeman would advise? You have read Noah Lukeman's *The First Five Pages: A Writers Guide to Staying Out of the Rejection Pile,* haven't you?

TWO WAYS TO START

In seminars I speak of two specific ways to begin a story. *Mise en Scene* and *In Media Res.* Conceptually, they work best when considering the length of your work, though a skilled writer can use either one regardless of genre or word count. But for most of us it is best to follow simple guidelines. So, long story or short?

MISE EN SCENE

Mise en Scene is a stage term meaning essentially to set the scenery. It offers a slower start and allows for the story to unfold. Generally it involves the description of the place or setting of the story and the reason the characters are there: mentally or physically or emotionally.

A pleasant aspect of using *Mise en Scene* includes the creative descriptions of the familiar and the way the writer uses language to set the tone of the tale. In a shorter story an author might feel the need to be more economical with description and scene setting. Trees might be bare and loom over park paths as the main character jogs in the early chill of winter. In using the *Mise en Scene* technique the trees may be arching their bare skeletal branches above cold paths, allowing pale sunlight to penetrate weakly into the park yet offering scant protection from ice-laden winds. Jogging in the early chill the main character may feel falsely protected in some minor way by the trees. Then a sliver of wind slices past the blood-red scarf loosely wrapped about her neck. In this second example the jogger may be experiencing some existential dread, as does the audience when offered the shading of the tone of language. Same scene essentially, but the beginning offers a separate experience.

In Media Res

In Media Res is more of a wakeup call. There is little scene setting and we get right into the action. When using this technique, I personally enjoy opening with a line of dialogue that is both compelling and slightly confusing for the reader. There is a school of thought that discourages this practice but done well it can propel your reader into the story quickly.

In both practices the first sentence sets not only the stage of the story but also the pace. You must make it all pay off, of course, and sooner rather than later or you will lose the reader. Give them a puzzling beginning but grant them solid clues as to where the tale is headed.

Mise en Scene is definitely a more useful concept if you are crafting a novel. When doing short stories, especially flash fiction, *In Media Res* is a skill necessary to master. The shorter the tale the less time and words you have to get the audience engaged, entertained, and satisfied. If the reader picks up a large book, they already know they are in for a longer commitment of time. There is a tacit agreement, and they will be more open and willing to allow for a slower, more leisurely paced genesis. Still, it is good to move them into the tale steadily. The pace may be slower, but it needs to be set and maintained with the idea of getting the reader to the conclusion.

WORDS TO REMEMBER

Beginnings are truly vital, but there must be a solid middle to sustain interest. What good is hooking a reader if they stop reading halfway through the story? It is a hungry fisherman who allows the fish to depart the hook while still in the sea. Half-read books are failures.

To make your story truly memorable, however, you must consider every word and sentence with equal importance. As you conceive the first lines, do you have the final lines in mind? A strong start is fine, but as anyone who participates in a foot race will tell you, a strong finish is necessary. What about the final five lines? Are they powerful enough to be remembered by your readers?

Consider the conclusion of *A Tale of Two Cities*. Good stuff, and memorable. *"It is a far, far better thing that I do, than I have ever done; it is a far, far better rest that I go to than I have ever known."*

Pretty good, don't you think? I believe this Dickens guy might have success as a writer.

"Writing a novel is like driving a car at night. You can only see as far as your headlights, but you can make the whole trip that way." ~ E. L. Doctorow

"And as imagination bodies forth, the forms of things unknown, the poet's pen turns them to shapes and gives to airy nothing, a local habitation and a name."
~ William Shakespeare (*A Midsummer Night's Dream*)

5

WHERE DO YOU GET YOUR CRAZY IDEAS?

"FROM WHENCE DOST WE DRAW BREATH?"

Sound like a cool quote? I just made it up. Out of thin air, as it were. I *respired* the words. The thought *expired* with a question mark. I whispered it to friend *conspiratorially*. It is an *inspiration* received. And of course, I am heavily intimating that the base of the word "spiros" (which might be Greek or maybe Latin…do I look like a scholar?) is also the basis for the word "spirit." Not like religion or Casper the Friendly, not Will Eisner's famous creation, or even 21-year-old Speyside Single Malt kind of spirit, but rather that intangible element that connects us to something…other. Something that might be us but is just outside. Something not physical, indefinable but present, and you know it when you sense it. That spirit.

Authors are often asked, "Where do you get your crazy ideas?" Many have a silly answer, some pithy, some wise and wonderful. The illusion is that they arrive unbidden - communique sent from above (or below in the case of horror writers) and that may be true. The truth is, more often than not, we conjure them like mediums claim to call spirits.

AN ALCHEMICAL REACTION

Inspiration is an alchemical reaction to input from our entire lives. We gain ideas from a vast mix of previously experienced words and images starting from before birth. What did mom and dad talk about after you were conceived? Those are the first words that have an effect on you, albeit perhaps a very minimal one. As creatives we take the leaden, commonplace communications and spin them into golden prose.

Reality time. Let us consider the fact that writers often are primarily inspired to write by other writers, other books, other stories told in various mediums. Not the kind of mediums that conjure spirits, but cinema, radio, poetry, or even music. Anything that tells a story we can access mentally and emotionally.

During an interview, I once asked science fiction/ fantasy author Gene Wolfe what question he was tired of getting when being interviewed. He said, "Where do you get your crazy ideas?" I then casually folded my notes over so that he could not see that my next question was, "Where do you get your crazy ideas?"

THERE IS NO SHORTCUT

Once upon a time, I was young enough to believe that if an author I admired told me their secret source of inspiration, perhaps I too could become a masterful creative artiste like my literary idols. You can't. There is no shortcut. You cannot walk another person's path and reproduce their artistic success.

Often what a writer will do is follow someone else's formula and produce some very similar version of their product. There is nothing wrong with doing this, and it is a fine way of making money. But if you are going for high-concept bold innovation and stunning creativity you must tap into your own connection to the universe. The universe itself is a creative energy and it is amazingly diverse in what it is accomplishing. In fact, I tell people that the universe does not support conformity, rather it encourages diversity in all aspects of itself.

You can feed your creative fire. You can seed the fields of your heart and brain with fertile and vital energies in the form of words and thoughts and familiar stories told in unique ways and unique stories told in familiar ways. Of course, you must till the soil, weed the crop, harvest and thresh the ripened yield, and if all that sounds like hard work, you are correct.

Getting the crazy idea for the story is often the easiest part, especially if you become adept at being open to inspiration.

THE SECRET

Here is the secret. It is worth the effort. After a field is harvested and gleaned, the community has food that nourishes and allows folks to survive and flourish. It is the same with stories. Stories feed us and feed our spirit. Humanity and the future are offered an opportunity to grow and evolve through the perpetual creation of stories told in whatever manner you, the author/creator doth choose.

And the other part of the secret? As one farmer's crop is essentially the same as another's, your book, song, or film is always a story that has been told before. It is only a new twist or style or rhythm that makes it seem fresh. While new recipes and combinations can help us enjoy the same old foods, there is something comforting in a meal made the same way your mother made it and her mother before. But she probably tweaked the recipe somewhere down the line.

READ GOOD WRITING

Mister Wolfe also told me that if I wanted to become a good writer, I need to read good writing. I pass that advice on to you in the hope that one day I will be reading your excellent and inspired storytelling.

Below I have included some lists of what I consider to be inspirational books for authors.

INSPIRATIONAL BOOKS ABOUT WRITING

- *On Writing* by Stephen King. The best book King ever wrote - just don't take everything he says as an absolute. Styles shift and alter. Few things are etched in stone.
- *Bird by Bird* by Anne Lamott. Sometimes referred to as an instruction manual, this is a clever, witty, and deeply insightful book, filled with lessons disguised as entertainment wrapped in skilled examples of fine writing.
- *Stealing Fire from the Gods* by James Bonnet. A treatise on the nature of STORY; absolutely essential for those who are seeking a deeper understanding of the nature and purpose of

storytelling. Read this book before you sign up for any expensive writing course.

- *Write Your Novel from the Middle* by James Scott Bell. Easy and brief with excellent observations about avoiding the muddle in the middle by starting there. More or less. For Pantsers and Plotters alike.

- *The First Five Pages* by Noah Lukeman. Another one that gets quoted a lot BUT…read it yourself and take away the principles and leave the rigid rules behind.

- *Save the Cat* by Blake Snyder. More of a book about screenwriting, but the principles apply to all storytelling mediums. The late Blake Snyder's Beat Sheets changed the world of writing.

FICTION THAT WILL INSPIRE YOU TO BE A BETTER WRITER

- *Tarzan of the Apes* by Edgar Rice Burroughs. An unexpected and literate story well told. Pure raw creativity. Forget what you think you know about Tarzan.

- *Replay* by Ken Grimwood. A metaphysical treatise on free will, choice, and destiny all told in an entertaining manner. Deeply, spiritually meaningful without sermonizing.

- *Time and Again* by Jack Finney. An atypical Time Travel story. The characters drive the tale.

- *Eva Luna/The Stories of Eva Luna* by Isabel Allende. The first book is the fictional life of a writer from birth to adulthood. The second contains the stories she writes allowing us to witness the influences of her life as informed by events in the first volume.

- *Swordspoint* by Ellen Kushner. Elegant writing, subtle world building, complex character arcs, and realistic romance, intriguingly clothed in fantasy style, accomplished without fantasy tropes.

- *M*A*S*H* by Richard Hooker. Satire by episode and ensemble cast on the nature of war and the sense of insanity, well communicated through madcap humor. Concise and sharp. It might be sacrilege to suggest this book is better than *Catch 22* by Heller, so I will not.

- *If On A Winter's Night A Traveler* by Italo Calvino. A truly meta construct of a novel. Is the reader of the book the true protagonist?

- *Always Coming Home* by Ursula K. LeGuin. A unique reading experience. Indescribably beautiful collection of interconnected stories, poems, notes, and more.

- *Soldier in the Mist* by Gene Wolfe. A brilliant twist on the unreliable narrator before anyone knew there was such a thing. Note: the phrase "A brilliant twist" can be applied to most all of Wolfe's writing. Read Gene Wolfe. Right now.

- *Neverwhere* by Neil Gaiman. I could just as easily say *Stardust* or the "Sandman" graphic novel series, but this one is the most accessible and remains one of the more brilliant ideas and interpretations of Gaiman's particularly poetic style. For absolute riotous fun also read *Good Omens,* co-written by Neil with Terry Pratchett. That is, "Sir Terry" and while you are at it, read this prolific, witty, astoundingly erudite fellow as well.

CLASSICS THAT INSPIRED EVERYTHING BEING WRITTEN TODAY

- *Frankenstein* by Mary Shelley. The mother of modern science fiction. Structure of Flashback
- *Dracula* by Bram Stoker. The father of modern horror and suspense. Structure of letter writing
- *The Time Machine/War of the Worlds* by H.G. Wells. The father of modern Science Fiction. Social ideas expressed in riveting tales of suspense and wonder

- *Hamlet* by William Shakespeare. Dialogue and quotable lines! Shakespeare gave us modern English.

- *20,000 Leagues Under the Sea* by Jules Verne. The father of modern adventure and fantastic fiction. Thousands of ideas within just one novel. *The Mysterious Island* invented the modern sequel. For better or worse.

- *Huckleberry Finn* by Mark Twain. The "father of American Literature" claims William Faulkner and who am I to disagree? Hemingway said *Huckleberry Finn* was the source of all American Literature, hence my choice of titles, but, like Gene Wolfe, just read Twain, any and all. You will grow as a writer.

- *The King of Elfland's Daughter* by Lord Dunsany. Pure fantasy and superior prose.

- *The Man Who Would Be King* by Rudyard Kipling. A short story with great power. I almost chose *Puck of Pook's Hill* which, if you are a fantasy writer, you should read immediately. "An immense gift for using words," T.S. Eliot said of Kipling, adding that he was, "a writer impossible wholly to understand and quite impossible to belittle." Like Twain and Wolfe, reading Kipling is a lesson that will guarantee growth and increased skill for a writer.

"If a man comes to the door of poetry untouched by the madness of the Muses, believing that technique alone will make him a good poet, he and his sane compositions never reach perfection, but are utterly eclipsed by the performances of the inspired madman." ~ Socrates

"We are all apprentices in a craft where no one ever becomes a master." ~ Ernest Hemingway

6

WRITES OF SUMMER

SELF-DISCIPLINE AND NECESSARY DISTRACTIONS

ONE OF THE HARSHEST REALITIES for me to come to terms with once I was out of the school system was that there was no longer a summer vacation scheduled into my life. "You mean, I have to show up for work…like every day?" I asked my supervisors disbelievingly. Many decades later I am still a bit miffed by this weird fact of life.

It is said that the goal of most of mankind is to be gainfully unemployed. This is why many of us choose to be writers. And for the most part it works for us. Except for that gainfully bit.

We authors seek greater freedom of time and a loosening of constraints of responsibility. Just like summer vacation in school days. But lack of structure and self-discipline soon becomes the downfall of many.

NO FREEDOM WITHOUT SELF-DISCIPLINE

It is said that there can be no freedom without self-discipline. Of course, the folks that say that are generally referring to a greater governmental philosophy beginning with Ancient Greece. Or maybe the Atlanteans.

In any case, as a writer who desires to be a published author, we must be prepared to work every day and eschew freedom of time for the tyranny of self-employment. I wince at my own words because I am not naturally inclined to any form of discipline.

In my experience, a creative being is rarely so inclined to act within the bounds of a traditional concept of self-discipline and structure. It is often those with a fair amount of entrepreneurial spirit that succeed over those with pure artistic genius. Please note: This is not a dissing of entrepreneurs. Only an acknowledgement of their skill set being the more successful business model.

DISTRACTIONS

The average human can be distractible. In the case of creative beings, they are eminently distractible.

Having deadlines put in front of them is annoying and may even be paralyzing. Setting of goals is anathema to many. Yet, without some structuring even the most brilliant writing will lie fallow on a shelf to be tossed out after the would-be brilliant author shuffles off this mortal coil. The genius-level tome falls under the "not to be" category, Shakespearally speaking.

Thus Seshat, the Egyptian Goddess of writers, created editors. Or maybe it was Baalat of Byblos. Personally, I am blessed with a wise and structured partner of the astrological sign of Taurus. She keeps this Gemini grounded (most of the time. With great effort, she adds).

But is it a distraction or are we feeding the Muse? Are we Pantsing or Plotting? It is a fine and wavy line that gets crisscrossed easily and often. Not unlike those Bump 'em cars at the county faire with the unreliable, but still present steering mechanism we writers wander mentally (and sometimes physically) in a creative haze. Itself hypnotic and if we are not careful, lazy making. Like the days of summer when we would just lie down in the shade of the old oak tree or sunbrella and doze the day away, the heat of pressure offered by deadlines can make us attain some kind of, "oh well, fiddle-dee-dee. I'll worry about it tomorrow" coma.

The question becomes, not "to be or not to be," but "will you or won't you." Recall that moment in late May when you made plans for the summer with classmates? Now recall that moment in late August when you realized that school started in a week!

And just to further complicate the plot and add some tension, mom said, "We have to go school supply shopping today, clothes shopping tomorrow, haircut getting next day and registration and pictures the day after that and don't forget this weekend we go to Aunt Ethels." You look out the window with dismay because you have not even called your friends, let alone fulfilled any well-intentioned plans. Clearly this is a coming-of-age story that probably does not apply to modern day cell phone texting civilizations, but hey! What a good evocation of my past!

The more disciplined a person was/is the more likely they also had a summer job and savings account. The less surprised they were by the lack of summer vacation time granted when they gained a career in a high-rise office and crafted reports and did accounting and stuff. Stuff like editorial work and publishing and contracts for writers.

We all are part of the food chain in this manner. Current society indicates that the creative must be part business and there is rub. For as soon as the creative begins writing for a market, they began manufacturing product that looks like other existing successful product. What sells?

Zombies sell. Jane Austen pastiches sell. Historical personages realistically portrayed in alternate universe setting sell. Pride and Prejudice and Zombies is a real book. As is Abraham Lincoln Vampire Hunter. The reviews are good (mostly). Are they great art? Great Literature? To Be Remembered and studied by future MFA candidates alongside Odysseus and Ulysses? No.

Are they useful distractions for the people who have nine to five jobs or work retail hours in holiday seasons? Yes. Fun books for busy people will always sell. Look at the romance market, say the entire line of Harlequin books. Look at the many permutations of mystery or thrillers, the many children of Christie or Le Carre.

And these all have one thing in common. They were finished.

Can you be a successful writer and make great art? Yes. But that field is narrow. It requires you to pay attention to your own personal calendar. August comes at us one day at a time.

"In the name of God, stop a moment, cease your work, look around you." ~ Leo Tolstoy

"When ideas come, I write them; when they don't come, I don't." ~ William Faulkner

"If you don't have time to read, you don't have the time (or the tools) to write. Simple as that."
 ~ Stephen King

7

THE COST OF FREEDOM

CREATIVES LOVE TO DREAM of being free. Free to paint, free to write, free to pursue any and all aspects of our abundant artistic dreams.

There is an old expression, probably someone like Thomas Jefferson or Alexis de Tocqueville said it: *Freedom isn't free.*

Crosby, Stills, Nash, and Young said, *"Find the cost of freedom, buried in the ground."* Okay, that second quote is depressing and really, we are not talking about dying for our art. But are we willing to live for creative expression? Most writers just want to make a living and not have to wear a shirt with their name printed on it. The point is that creatively driven beings seek an outlet and we will find it no matter what our circumstances.

SACRIFICES MADE FOR FREEDOM

At a recent writers' conference in San Diego, I spoke with an aspiring author who said that in seeking time to write he gets up at three in morning, before his wife and children rise, before he needs to shower and get ready to go to his accounting job. Before his "real life" begins, he says. He has a specific ritual that he conducts before sitting down to the computer and part of it is noisy enough that it can be heard in the bedroom. It is a scientific fact that coffee makers are louder in the middle of the night. His wife agrees to ignore this in support of his writing efforts.

At that same conference I met a working mom with an excellent concept for a novel. She stays awake until one in the morning, after all the work is accomplished: dishes washed and put away, lunches made for the next day, bills and household accounting completed, as well as herding her three boys towards their bedroom. Then, and only then, will she sit and enter the world she is creating. It is a hopeful world; one she desires to offer to others who seek a better future for their children. Her husband helps a lot, she says, but admits there is a control freak aspect where she needs to know that everything is done RIGHT — that is, to her satisfaction — before she can relinquish her grip on the household responsibilities. She finally gave up trying to get the boys to wear matching pajama bottoms and tops and now allows dad to handle bedtime.

CHOICES

We all have our quirks and responsibilities. We also make our choices. The absolute need to create is something that can be denied for a time. Like food. But often the necessity overcomes the perceived limitations and will burst forth and not be deterred.

The price to pay for the time spent can be a derogation of duties. Sometimes it is a dereliction of duties. The man in the example above is the husband to the woman who goes to bed after midnight. They have bargained, negotiated, and agreed to a specific organizing of tasks, and more importantly recognize and respect one another's particular weirdnesses and compulsions. They grant one another space and understanding and assist in the gift of freedom. But they pay the price. And they are each close to completing their prospective projects.

Will they make a living at their book writing? Or will he need to continue bookkeeping to sustain the level of income necessary for them to live in Southern California? Again, the cost is considered, and they have chosen to adjust their lives to allow for creative expression.

Why Did I Wait?

Many writers don't actually begin their work in earnest until they near retirement. "All the time in the world," says one published gentleman. "And it is all the same time I had all my life, I just made different choices as to what to do after work. Why did I wait?"

Truth to tell, there may be reasons to wait. Creativity can be dampened. Mental weariness is not conducive to creative activity. Emotional exhaustion can legitimately deter the process of expressing deep-seated, heartfelt communications between characters undergoing traumatic circumstances.

Writers and artists operate in a vacuum. They often experience deep insecurities about their abilities. Participation in a community is difficult when time must be spent making a living. Part of the cost of writing is dealing with your own foibles and phobias.

There is a certain courage necessary. Remember that the word courage has, as its roots the term "cor," Latin for "heart." All true, creative artistic effort stems from the emotional core of an individual. Passion for a project will propel success and completion far more effectively than seeking profit.

PASSION AND PROFIT

This is not to say that profit should not be sought. Every action has an opposite and equal reaction. If you produce a quality product, there will be an equivalence of return on your investment. It may not be in the form of income, coin, or currency. But there is no crime in going for the gold. Your cost may be the lessening of your artistic intent to create a more commercially viable final result. You are free to make that choice.

The current world of digital media accessibility is vast. The opportunity to experience success is wide open. Creating an eBook is practically free. But there is more content being produced today than ever before. You, the writer, are in competition with everything being created today and everything that has come before. This means more effort required and more time spent. Not in creating but in marketing, the tooting of one's own horn. For many the choice is difficult, not because they do not want to create, but because there are so many shiny objects that can distract our questing and curious artistic souls.

And then there is Free Cell.

Freedom is not free. The price to living a fulfilling life is the decision to use our time wisely.

"Excellence is never an accident. It is always the result of high intention, sincere effort, and intelligent execution; it represents the wise choice of many alternatives - choice, not chance, determines your destiny." ~ Aristotle

"I love deadlines. I like the whooshing sound they make as they fly by." ~ Douglas Adams

8

IN THE HEAT
OF THE MOMENT

CREATIVE INSPIRATION cannot consistently be turned on and off, like a faucet. It strikes in the oddest of moments: the shower, the drive to work, the middle of the night, or during a movie that just is not holding your attention. As a writer we need to strike while the iron is hot. What does that expression even mean? It means that when forging a tool or weapon the blacksmith would spend a great deal of time creating a very specific kind of fire and select a specific ingot of metal. After inserting the metal into the forge fire, the smith tended the fire and coals and turns the metal to and fro, allowing heat to permeate evenly and soften even the hardest of metals. All this was in preparation for the work to be accomplished. But when all was in readiness, when the iron was at the perfect stage of malleability, the mighty smith would take his hammer and…yes, you know the rest.

Have you, as an author or artist, felt that sudden burst of inspiration? Have you ever sat down at the keyboard and felt words pouring out in a blaze of white-hot creativity? Have you ever been "on fire" with ideas and execution? Have you ever sat at your computer and stared at the screen in utter dismay wondering – "Where is the creative energy and why has my muse abandoned me?" Too often I hear the latter lament. The secret?

STRIKING WHILE THE IRON IS HOT

Striking while the iron is hot is not always a random event. Sure, you get those bursts which occur at the most inconvenient moments. I once heard of a writer who accessed a sudden vison of her entire novel while in the middle of her own wedding ceremony. Tough to scribble notes when you are taking vows. The initial ideas were sketched out in the ladies' room on the backs of cake napkins, and then entrusted to her bridesmaid. By the way, the marriage did not last, but the book is pretty good.

The truth is, you have your own forge and your own fire to tend and stoke. There are materials waiting for you and you cannot simply rely on blinding flashes of brilliance to sustain your career. The metal must be examined prior to the forging. Designs must exist. Skills must be learned and honed. It is not enough for a craftsman to make a blade. Understanding the end purpose of it will enhance its quality. A smithy can often wield the tools he crafts in addition to his own tools. You must know your trade. The blacksmith does not approach a cold anvil and forge and wait for inspiration. He also does not wait for lightning to strike and heat up the metal.

It is the same with any creative endeavor. And by creative I don't simply mean art. Designing and building a house is creative. So is building a business. Planting crops and raising animals is creative. All these things require forethought and knowledge. Often in the pursuit of knowledge we discover a new way of doing things. We gain insight and with it feel inspiration. And suddenly, or so it seems, we are in the heat of the moment. The fever is upon us, and we feel a surge of energy.

This is called synergy, the creation of something greater than the simple elements used in bringing the project to existence. It is the use of letters to form words, then using the words to form sentences, and crafting the sentences and paragraphs to express deep emotion and high philosophical concepts. The collecting of the elements happens constantly. The more aware a writer is regarding the world around them and the more aware of the concerns of others, the greater the scope of the tale they can create using basic skills they gained in school.

ENCOURAGING YOUR MUSE

But first, always first, we must be prepared to be possessed by the muse, to release our self-imposed limitations and allow for a free flow of concepts and ideas. It helps if we have a ritual or habitual space and time that we approach our forge, the place where we have banked the fire and the coals never cool - that space where creativity always occurs. And when we arrive it feels like the seat is already warm and waiting.

Seize moments of random inspiration by all means. Keep a notepad and pencil near you at all times just in case. Be surreptitious if you must. Bathroom stalls are great notetaking spots. Who is going to interrupt or question your absence from any gathering if you are in the privy? But if you desire to be the hottest new author, you must cultivate consistent heat.

I delight in the myth of Prometheus. But I do so for entirely different reasons than when the story was first told. Sitting around a real fire, a storyteller would relate how this life-giving element of flame providing light and heat to the tribe in a controlled fashion came to them as a gift from a rebellious god. Prometheus brought fire to humanity and suffered for his actions, his sacrifice on our behalf. The gods did not want mankind to have control over such combustive power, the implication being that somehow humanity was perceived as unworthy by the gods and should remain in an animalistic state.

In our day and age, the myth takes on a different element. It is not so much the actual flame that we have been given, but in a cumulative way the original fire has led us to greater enlightenment through creating a life not limited to daylight hours and spring and summer growth. We now read and study by the light carried forward from ancient times.

Centuries of study and pondering lessons of the past now offer us a figurative enlightenment. The sense of Promethean sacrifice is rooted in the rebellion of questioning what the gods, those who are nominally "in charge" of the world, want hidden from our sight.

Our stories warm us and bring perception to dark places. The light source may be different, screens instead of campfires, candles, or gaslight, yet here we are, telling stories and passing on wisdom, thanks to the creative Promethean enlightenment. As a creative being, will you waste such a flame, or fan it to brilliant, white-hot purifying art?

9

YIN AND YANG
OF STORYTELLING

IN MUCH OF THE 20th CENTURY, stories were often based in a good versus evil setting. As if the world were that simple. One hero, one villain, and voila! They struggle and fight and often the hero is simple and pure while the villain is just mean for the sake of being mean.

In our 21st Century world where audiences have been subjected to reviewers and critics since birth (I blame Siskel and Ebert for making us hyper-aware of the storytelling techniques and tropes in common use), it is increasingly difficult to get away with telling a tale that is just bad guy versus good guy and let the fight begin.

Eastern philosophy presents us with the principles of Yin and Yang. They are the active aspects and energies of balance and harmony in the universe. In the west, we have often simplified this concept as dark and light, male and female, or good and evil. This doesn't actually work for more reasons than we will discuss here, but a brief examination of the philosophy may increase your ability as a writer to craft a more complex and balanced story.

Yang more easily and accurately translates as action or structure, perhaps even as logic. Yin translates as peaceful or creative, emotional satisfaction, or as I say, the heart's desire.

WE ARE NOT DEALING WITH OPPOSITES

Although the symbolization of yin and yang is delineated as two equal but separate shapes, within each shape is an element of the other. A circle of Yang within Yin, and a space of Yin within Yang.

If you have a character that is quite logical, they must also possess a bit of emotional strength to be complete. Conversely, a person who is highly emotional will be more interesting if they seek to nurture some logic or structure within their lives. A character bound in one dimension is stagnant. But if that same logical character has a secret desire to be an artist or engage in some form of creative endeavor, acting against the rules of their society, you have, as a storyteller, opened up a deeper level of conflict within your story.

If your story has a character who is a wild and crazy artist, a person who possesses absolutely no structure or limits in their life, how does that affect their society? They might even be viewed as a villain by some of the other characters if they leave chaos in their wake. But if they are doing so out of rebellion against strict rules or fundamentalist laws, if they are secretly desirous of an orderly life, one where they might be happy with themselves and then, perhaps another, a partner, then the inner conflict spices the outer scenario and intensifies the storyline.

The days of one-dimensional (or single-faceted) villains Hans Gruber and Goldfinger ("He loves only gold.") have passed us by for the most part. In our world we know enough psychology to understand that the villains have feelings too. The agenda they create has a purpose, even if they must use nefarious or antisocial means to gain their goal.

Our story and movie heroes transformed earlier than their villainous counterparts. Our somewhat flawed Bruce Willis' John McClain and various James Bonds lack the purity of the older cowboy film stars or super heroic serials of Flash Gordon and Superman. Their imperfections work in allowing us, the audience, to engage more fully with the characters. They could be us! The flaws also allow us, as writers, to more easily create intriguing tales based on the twilight area between the brightest day and the blackest night.

Never underestimate your audience's ability to grasp complex motivations. It may not be that they are doing so consciously, but the principles of Yin and Yang hold true in every level of life. It is the seeking of a balance that drives the best stories.

10

WRITING SCARED

YOU ARE ALONE. The only light in the room shines directly into your eyes. You are faced with questions, intense questions, with persistent demands for answers. You do not know all the answers. Sometimes you do not know why the questions are being asked. The room behind you has one shadow, your own, cast upon the wall by the terrible light of the computer screen. You are a writer, and it is sometimes the hardest and scariest job in the world. We fear many things as writers, but mostly we fear ourselves or perhaps, what we truly fear is our sanity!

Should you call the authorities on yourself? Does everyone have voices in their head? Are they answering you right now?

You may think: *Where did that weird and unstable thought come from? My character is a villain, certainly, but that? That is grotesque and disturbing! Hmmm. Perhaps I should google it and see how this depraved thing is actually accomplished...*

It is not always villainy. Sometimes it is simply basic human relationships. But, Oh! How twisted they can become!

Oh my! That is so sad! He is so demeaning and treats my poor heroine so badly! Why would any man do such a thing to a woman, especially such a handsome, virile, successful man that she is so clearly in love with and they are the perfect match made in...wait a sec! This is a sick, sad relationship! How can I write such a passive-aggressive story? Where does this come from within my own psyche? Certainly I am not like this, am I? Maybe if I keep on writing for a while Rod Strong will see Emma Worthing's desperate loveliness and fall in deep and abiding love and they will love each other until...It never dies! (Ooohhh! Good title! Love Never Dies) Yes! He can change and he WILL!

MANY TWISTED THOUGHTS
CAN ARISE WITHIN THE WRITER

We writers periodically joke at our own expense that we need someone to clear our document and browser history if we are ever tragically lost in the jungles of Cambodia searching for a lost temple, or perish in

Paris when an asteroid strikes and destroys most of the civilized world but miraculously leaves our laptop intact, or if the experimental prototype sub-orbital jet we are riding in for research for our next bestselling thriller accidentally launches itself into space and we are sent to spend our final days spinning into the sun...or if we are just incapacitated by some mundane occurrence like a broken leg. Of course, we only joke about this with other writers, preferably in our same genre. Preferably late at night in the sad, confessional nature of the hotel bar while we are attending a writers' conference where we meet other equally normal, but secretly twisted, folks.

But are we really twisted? Are we really so weird? Or is it that we give voice to others who have secret fears and bent psyches? Is it that the human experience is one that is fearful, and we simply observe the nature of society and report it, albeit in an entertaining way? And hopefully in a way that translates into sales.

Should the thought that we tap into dysfunctional relationships and make them appear common enough to discuss out loud over tea and crumpets scare us even more? *And what are crumpets anyway? Should I have used the word scones instead? No, this is a funny piece, not a mystery. Are you talking to yourself again?*

Truth is, the world is a dysfunctional mess most of the time and we, as writers, often transcend the judgment phase of society to try to comprehend the why of people's motivations. While transcending judgment, we simultaneously seek to look past the accepted narrative of societal mythology and create a greater awareness or raise perceptions higher than the mundane.

In a sense we place ourselves above the population and look down upon them, foolish mortals that they be, and we see the futility of their pathetic struggles and offer them insight and wisdom through our tales of derring-do and romance and bug-eyed monsters, even if they never comprehend the multifaceted depths of our ART. Yea, we behold their foibles and, and...sometimes get that god complex going at a high rate of speed. *But that isn't psychopathic, is it? More sociopathic, right, and that's not as bad, is it? Better Google that one...*

In our writing, specifically fiction and genre work, we sometimes use standardized tropes to craft a basic storyline, one that has been told many times before, but we personally inject our own observations of life through our varied characters' perceptions. In this we personally can make sense of why our family and friends act the way they do and why we react to them and then they react to us. It can be scary to be so intensely self-analytical. But it is liberating as well. Not just for the writer, but also for the audience.

Wait. You mean someone might actually read this stuff and then they might actually talk to me about it? What if the neighbors find out? What if my high school class, the ones I based most of my most depraved characters upon…what if they discover my bestselling book soon-to-be-a-major motion picture? Should I be using a pseudonym?

And here we pause because I have given myself writer's block.

THE SCARY THOUGHT OF ACTUALLY LETTING SOMEONE ELSE SEE YOUR WORK

The quiet is pervasive. Usually you are distracted by so many noises that it is difficult to concentrate on your Craft, your Profession, your burgeoning Career of being a Published Author. But you have closed every window, shut every door, scolded and cajoled every member of the family to silence and peace, including the dog. The only one that appreciates this is the cat, who now is supine across your keyboard, but even this rascal will tolerate being moved as long as it is only to your lap, and you offer occasional worship via gentle petting. Now you can really get some work done! Now you can hit that self-imposed, read it in a book, heard it from a successful author word count! NOW, Now, now you have a blank screen, staring at you unblinking, unnervingly, daring you to be great. Go ahead, I double dog dare you! Be brilliant right now! Write! NOW!

And you cannot even begin to remember the names of the characters you so carefully created out of whole cloth over the last year. Your outline seems to be written in Greek and you only speak Latin. The storyline is apparently that of Huck Finn complete with your heroes traveling down a river in search of gold, or love, or to stop the terrorists, or solve the mystery of the missing tea cozy…What? Tea cozy? You are an idiot. A complete fool who is no longer to be allowed to walk the streets in public. There is nothing brilliant about any of this mess and you are a fool on a fool's errand. You dare not let anyone see the dreck you haven't even bothered to write yet…

SIGH

You, my friend, are not a fool, an idiot, a reprobate, a mug, chump, or dupe. You are simply, like many writers, afraid. It is not that you lack talent. It is not the noise of others or the lack of noise. It is that there is noise in your head that sabotages your motion. It is the single thing that stops writers from ever completing a manuscript. And you are not alone, you only believe you are. John Cleese said, *"Nothing will stop you being creative so effectively as the fear of making a mistake."*

Nothing attributes to the fear of making a mistake more than the desire to be perfect the first time. Ego-driven writers will want their first draft to be viewed as pristine art. And most of us are ego driven when we first begin. We lose that ego through a scary process called revision and critique. But first is the scary first draft. This is where we make every mistake in the book *Get it? "In the book," right? Nudge, nudge.*

If you believe that only first-time writers get this fear of the blank page, you are mistaken. It is an easy mistake to make when you see certain authors turning out a book a year, or in some cases multiple books a year, and they are selling and speaking and having a great life drinking mojitos on the beach while they dictate brilliantly into a recording device which is hooked up via magic to a computer in a manly, brass-riveted, leather-furnitured, oak-paneled office or a sunny, glassed-in, feminine, garden-engulfed solarium, and the words spew forth from the mystically created document into a printer that never jams and always has full cartridges and no one, NO ONE, ever changes a word of the successful author's pure unadulterated genius.

Do not be deluded. Red ink is copiously used by ALL successful writers, specifically because they want to be successful. Yes, at first sight it does look like blood and suspiciously like your type, but a little bleeding is necessary in life. You must fall and skin your knees as a child before you walk and run. (Don't even get me started on the head wounds I suffered as a child learning to ride a bike! Head trauma is probably the root cause of the voices in my head!)

PERFECT IS THE ENEMY OF FINISHED

We never are perfect, especially the first time out. In the seeking of perfection, we again hobble ourselves.

Deep breath, my anxiety-ridden writerly friend. Just write. It will suck. Don't worry about it. Robert Kiyosaki said, "Don't waste a good mistake, learn from it." No one needs to see your first draft or the second or third. Feel that fear and do it anyway! The scariest part is yet to come!

Somewhere in time you will find it necessary to gain a support group of equally fearful folk who are seeking validation of their own efforts and want someone to recognize that they are geniuses waiting to be discovered. They band together in an insecure, self-defensive, ever-morphing form and call themselves a Critique Group (from the Old French for "Those who drink wine and comment endlessly on things they know little about").

Here within this village of those seeking to not be perceived as idiots you will receive opinions. Now I will tell you that the word EGO comes from the self-improvement, motivational-speaker wisdom that Everyone's Got Opinions. Equally I will point out that FEAR is an acronym that means False Expectations Already Realized. Or maybe it is Fail Early And Respond (responsibly).

The point is that a first draft finished is farther than most people ever get. And a second peer-reviewed draft and a third show that you are serious about the process. Your process. The word "process" sounds like progress if you squint and look at it with your head tilted. Writing a book is all about progress, not perfection.

LET'S TALK ABOUT CRITIQUE GROUPS

Critique groups. Never pleasant, always necessary. In a critique group you will hear your words as others do and you will, if you are in a semi-balanced and mostly sane critique group, hear how others think you can improve your work. In other words, their ego will confront your ego. And they will be in the same position of vulnerability because they too will be presenting their deathless prose for you to cast an opinion upon. Give good feedback and accept whatever feedback you receive, but do not internalize either. You are the creator of your story and the final arbiter of its worth. At least until you publish. Then the audience, the terrifying, ravening hordes of readers hungry to be entertained and amused will cast their eyes on your painstakingly crafted document of 50,000 to 100,000 meticulously crafted words and some will say, "I can write better than that!" but you, YOU are an AUTHOR and they are mere wannabe's sitting alone in front of a computer screen with an unblinking white light awaiting their first words and daring them to be brilliant.

ACKKK! You mean random strangers who I have never met will be able to write their own ego-based reviews and publish them for the ENTIRE WORLD to read! But I should explain my story to them before they read it! Maybe one more revision...

Sorry buckaroo. Published you are and it is time to move on to the next. The one you wanted to write all your life. The Great American Novel. NO! The Next GLOBAL Blockbuster Bestseller! And as you sit down to write your next book (and the next and on and on), that soon-to-be-familiar creeping dread begins to grow. For you perpetually face the next Scary First Draft.

11

THE GRATEFUL WRITER

A BRIEF HISTORY OF THE PRINTED WORD

I CANNOT THINK OF A BETTER TIME in history to be a writer. Sure, it is tough to make a living at it, but for those seeking the opportunity to become a published author, this is the authorial space age, baby! And a successful moon landing is within reach of everyone.

THE FIRST WRITERS

Think of it: After Cro-Magnons got out of their caves and decided they wanted to be able to transport the stories that they had been painting on cave walls, humanity started to create little bits of cuneiform-carved mud to record important events, like the selling of a goat for enough wheat to make Enkiduian amounts of beer. (And of course, the character of Enkidu got to have an epic meeting with heroic Gilgamesh in those proto books.)

Then one day, those ancestors discovered that processed plant pith and animal skins were much lighter and rolled up nicely around sticks. Papyrus and vellum put the cave painting business firmly into the history scrolls. Of course, if you were Pharaoh, you created your own caves and paintings but that was a nostalgic Luxor-y. It was important to master the new scrolling technology if you wanted to be included in the Library of Alexandria. And you are not a REAL writer if you're not still a little bit bummed about THAT nasty episode.

PENMANSHIP

Soon enough, paper evolved from papyrus, and paper pages became the latest and greatest advancement of the day. In the not-quite-as-old days, a writer wrote longhand on paper with pencil. They scratched out sentences that did not work, or rewrote paragraphs in the margins of their manuscript, so-called because it was Manually Scribed. *Late 16th cent.: from Medieval Latin manuscriptus, from manu 'by hand' + scriptus 'written' (past participle of scribere).*

Legibility mattered. The author needed to know how to communicate clearly using a skill called penmanship. I do not know if there was ever such a term as quillmanship. If a word was misspelled, the writer either had to possess the knowledge that it was wrong because they were well read and educated, or they relied on an editor to catch and correct any errors in spelling or grammar.

AN INDUSTRIAL REVOLUTION

As the industrial revolution created new machines that offered an easier, more convenient way to create and deliver a story, the would-be author once again had to up their game and knowledge of the technology. The long-suffering editor, however, would never again look at a hand-written manuscript after the advent of the typewriter.

The keyboard required every writer to know how to type and apply the correct format (and every single page needed to be formatted). If you did not use carbon paper, then there was only one copy of your work. If that were lost your time was spent attempting to recreate your book from scratch. Then a second copy needed to be typed and submitted to the editor and publisher, who bloodied your hard copy with their brutal red pens, thereby necessitating yet another rewrite (re-type) and the creation of a third, fourth, and probably a fifth draft. Many writers became known for their alcoholic consumption when they were asked to create a fifth draft. Get it? Fifth? Draft?

Each draft was sent by mail with appropriate postage plus return postage, and then wait, wait, wait. The invention of the SASE is likely to be a forgotten bit of history, but it was vital to the process. A self-addressed stamped envelope was required if you wanted a response. Sometimes, oftentimes, the SASE didn't matter. You still never heard from the publisher again and must assume that your laboriously written book was now merely slush pile matter.

If you ever received a rejection letter it was almost a relief, because then you knew that someone somewhere read your words and made a judgment about them. But why was it rejected? "Your work does not fit our needs at this time," was the most probable response.

TRADITIONAL PUBLICATION IS BORN

If you were fortunate, and did your homework, and appealed to a person likely to be interested in your style or genre, you might actually gain a critique with the rejection. This could be exciting! This meant that someone took the time to attempt to nurture you, and that your book actually captured their interest. A relationship could be developed, and years may pass, but eventually, against outstanding odds, you may gain a contract! They would then ask what you were currently working on, and you would think, "I'm working on getting this manuscript published and making a million bucks," but the publisher was already seeking a follow-up. You would then sit with a pad of paper and pencil and the process would once again begin.

Within recent memory, people began going to college to gain a Bachelor of Arts degree in English, an MFA, or some literature-related study to gain the necessary knowledge to become an author. What they often gained was a degree in how to get traditionally published and support the traditional path to publication.

In other words, they were able to supplement their earnings as a writer with a real job as an editor or reviewer or magazine contributor or even as a teacher, teaching the traditions. Credentials meant legitimacy and offered relief from the dread tag of "self-published" being assigned to your soon-to-be obscure book.

And then science fiction happened. Y2K came and went, and it was wonderful. The computers failed to self-destruct, and the world evolved into the internet. Look what hath been wrought!

THE MAGIC BOX

As a lousy typist (but a would-be storyteller and successfully published author), I find myself eternally grateful to the vexing and oft times problematic technology of the 21st Century. Just the fact that I EXIST in the 21st Century is a type of science fiction to the ten-year-old me. Certainly technology has failed me on the personal-rocket-pack scale, but I am perpetually astounded by the vast array of content available to me wherever I find myself on the planet. Every form of research or fact I desire is just a magic, finger-swipe away.

I now have the ability to make notes using electronic document programs available to me on my phone (aka the magic box) either by typing on a virtual keyboard or by using my voice. The latter more often than not yields some writing of dubious literary value, but hey, crappy first draft by voice is still sci-fi to the kids in the 1950s.

Today, using a machine that fits on your lap, you can write, edit, submit to critique groups, commune and commiserate with fellow struggling writers, and then when no agents or publishers respond to your well-crafted website and platform, you can turn to Create Space or any other myriad formats for Self-Publishing (I mean INDIE publishing) and within a matter of days cobble together a cover, gain an ISBN number, and publish straight to the awaiting audience. Will it suck? Is it genius? You won't know until you put your work out there. Is it legitimate? By the measuring stick of ever-increasing sales or personal satisfaction, YES!

THE DEMOCRATIC PROCESS

In our times a book can happen in days rather than years. We have a world that says everyone, with a certain amount of savvy, can now be published authors. Is this a good thing or not? That is a philosophical debate. Is it the ultimate in democratic, everyone-gets-a-voice society? Yes, pretty much it is, along with the internet discussion threads. Will anyone read or listen to your words? Up to you, mostly. You still have to have platform and publicity and reviews on Amazon and pay attention to sales and ranking algorithms and such stuff that causes most creative souls to cringe and whimper.

But aren't you grateful that you live now, rather than at the time of the invention of the printing press? Inking a text block can be so messy.

And did I mention spell check? Yeah, now you're feeling grateful!

"Yes, there is a Nirvanah; it is leading your sheep to a green pasture, and in putting your child to sleep, and in writing the last line of your poem."

~ Kahlil Gibran

"Write your story as it needs to be written. Write it honestly, and tell it as best you can. I'm not sure that there are any other rules. Not ones that matter."

~ Neil Gaiman

12

THE GIFT OF THE IMAGI

IMAGINATION, A GIFT SHARED

THERE ARE TIMES I PINE FOR THE WORLD THAT WAS. A strange nostalgia sweeps over me, and I do not understand the why of it all. I feel deeply that I should be living in another age, another part of the world, or as a completely different personality. Past life memories? Perhaps.

Perhaps it is due to the story I just read, the one that compelled me to remain awake deep into the early morning hours despite a tiring day. I ignored my chores and canceled my plans of getting outside to exercise. Okay, it doesn't have to be that compelling to get me to ignore exercise or delay taking the garbage out, but you get my point. You have been there before. I hope.

These modern days, it is not so common a thing to be captivated by mere words: the images conjured from ink and paper, the weaving of phrases and rhythmic parsing of paragraphs into a swelling tale of emotional risk and reward, the catch in one's throat when realizing, in the final pages, where the story leads. Have you wept at the conclusion of a book? While reading, have you laughed out loud in the midst of strangers on a train or plane? Have you felt joy and fear for a character that exists only in images – spells cast through language and into your thoughts…through imagination?

ARE WE ALONE?

Do other creatures tell stories to one another? I have found no evidence of this, and the general conclusion is that there is no such phenomenon clearly attributable to cetaceans or primates beyond Homo sapiens. This does not rule it out, of course. It could be that the stories they tell are incomprehensible to humanity, that we simply do not perceive their manner. Or perhaps the noble silverback gorillas or ocean-going dolphins do not deem us worthy audiences to learn of their great histories or deep genetic memories.

Do other creatures even have imagination? Is this a singular gift we alone, we Homo sapiens, we storytellers, have been allowed through a creator or by evolutionary action?

Can you imagine a life on earth without being able to use your imagination? A life with no stories, no books, no songs, or no cinema with its fantastic, flickering images holding visual memories from the dawn of photography and film?

Can you pause for a moment and IMAGINE how blessed we actually are to possess this sense, this perceptive capability?

A GENEROUS PASSION

Writers and storytellers create entire worlds, entire societies, entire scenarios, dramatic and comedic, that seek and invite others to enter within and gain experiences they may never have. Space travel, time travel, global travel, emotional travel, journeys through figurative and literal landscapes that are mirrors of our own reality. Then we proceed to step out and share our words with the rest of our species, to give back and spread our stories in our communities, local and global.

We share our personal gifts of perception and emotion for a variety of reasons, true. Some for profit, some for fame, some for posterity. But each crafter of a tale, each weaver of words, each spell caster of fictional events and historical occurrences is ultimately a generous gift giver to our often-anonymous readers who bear witness to the imagined activities we record.

As such, we authors stand in a long line of tribal odd fellows. Like shamans, or medicine men and women, we are the strange member of the community who stays awake and watches the skies and observes the stars. We are the moon gazers who offer myth and legend to explain and carry lessons for the benefit of the whole village, for the survival of the coming generations, perhaps, but also to pass the time around the fires, whether wood, coal, or electronic.

A UNITED COMMUNITY

No matter what form the light that keeps the dark away, the stories impel the tribe to remain close together. We are stronger together. Or they may tell us of those who went off on their own, whether by choice or by tragic accident, separated from their familiar surroundings and friends, and how they used their bravery and wits to not only survive, but flourish and ultimately return to the world.

The teller of the tale is completed by those who are practical, who accomplish the tasks that allow for daily life to continue. The hearers of the tales perpetuate the current societies by building houses, farming foods we consume, and transporting goods for the tribe to enjoy. They are the audience, the ones who need and desire the words we weave. We are united by the images conjured and perceived.

And when we ourselves are touched by a story, a book or film, we feel that rush of jealousy, admiration, wonder, and desire to increase our own ability. We reach for the goal of having a similar effect on others. As authors and creatives, we may strive for new, superior techniques that separate our tale from the past and make us unique, yet we are the culmination of our art only for the generation we exist within. The ones that follow, those that may read our words long after we have exited the planet, will build on the works and styles and patterns, and craft their own, birthing relatable tales for the society they live in. Just as we do. Just as our predecessors have done.

A UNIVERSAL CONNECTION

We are storytellers, and we are connected to the universe by the state of imagination, that strange gift of creative energy.

We can say thank you to those who went before us, those we know of and those we know existed but who remain forever anonymous in the mists of wood-fire smoke and time.

And we can look forward, imagining and encouraging those who will take up the torch after we're gone, the storytellers of the future who will give back to their communities with the words they weave, who will guide and entertain and educate those future generations we will never know.

EPILOGUE
I DON'T WISH TO SPOOK YOU, BUT...

...BEING A WRITER IS A SCARY LIFE. I am haunted by books not written and ideas long forgotten. Where did that moment of brilliance go that I experienced while walking to the store to buy a lottery ticket? I failed to write it down! I possessed no piece of paper or writing implement! Now it has fled my mind, that melding of thought and emotion where creativity attains structure. Alas! I have failed in the respect that one precious concept is vanished, like a ghost in daylight. This happens to me frequently.

Some days the ideas come so rapidly, rising like Dracula and his brides from the graveyard near Carfax Abbey. It is frightening. Yet, like dead leaves in an autumnal wind, I let them blow past. One cannot pursue every idea even with the suspicion that it has hidden secret value. Life is too short. Death befalls us all. We mere mortals must struggle to leave our mark on the world, perhaps attain literary immortality by pursuing one solitary story to its imminent completion before it eludes us like a phantom in the deepening shadows of the sewers below the opera house.

The scary part is how many times I hear published authors say that they have too many ideas, a crypt of notes, decaying scrolls of past thoughts, a tomb of tomes birthed and abandoned: first lines, character names, settings and situations that might make for an excellent story. Yet they never chose just one and thus nevermore are quoted by readers or ravens. Their legacy of papers perishes with them in funeral pyre, as their heirs battle over dark earthen material inheritances of gold and silver, leaving abandoned all intellectual property.

It is equally terrifying when I hear people who want to be writers, who claim ONE great idea and they are willing to share it with me or some other published author if only we will write it for them, do the actual digging work and exhume all the valuables this wannabe knows are buried in their valuable concept. "Please Mr. King, Mr. Clancy," they plead, "WE will make a million on this idea of mine. And all you have to do is the easy part. Just type out the details."

Inevitably the story is one that has been told before, dusty and cobwebbed, but with some terrifyingly inane twist. "It is like cowboys, but in space. With dinosaurs!" And they are willing to sell their soul, er, sole literary property, to gain life at the expense of another's lifeblood. "But writing is so easy," they may say, to which I will agree and misquote Red Smith and Paul Gallico who said something frighteningly similar to one another, "Writing is easy. Just open a vein and bleed on the page."

"Where do you get all your crazy ideas?" some will ask, and in truth it is a common interview question, one that causes dread in an author's heart. Such is the despair some feel at the posing of the question that they prepare a pat answer, designed to be sly and sharp witted enough to drive a stake through any follow-up query on the subject. Because the big secret, hidden within a dank, dark lair in the fevered brain of the mad scientist-like writer is…ideas are easy, a dime a dozen. It is the translation of those concepts into heartfelt tales of love won or lost, destinies achieved, enemies conquered or converted to allies, mistakes amended and atoned, monsters destroyed or socially re-adjusted, all brought to clarity through the use of language and storytelling craft; it is the process of creation to completion that is horribly, terrifyingly maddening in its isolation. The accompanying self-doubt is rumored to be the primary cause of mournful midnight moon howling.

Writing is a solitary pursuit. If you fear the empty room, choose a different path. If a blank page that calls out in sepulchral tones, wailing for your words, sends blood-chilling spasms through your corporeal form, I beg of you, do not walk into that Borgo Pass of shadowed life. But if it is your wont to creep about in the midnight hours, prowling dusty shelves of forgotten libraries, seeking secrets of bringing beings to life, whether through spells found in the Egyptian Book of the Dead, the use of Tana leaves (three or nine, your choice) or simply having a quiet cup of tea alone in the light of the full moon, then gather those ideas that leap at you unexpectedly from the weird corners of your subconscious, your misunderstood Id and Super-Ego, whispering absolutely nutty things into your bat-eared alter-ego and get thee to a raven-feathered quill or Alienware laptop!

When you have achieved that first draft, when you feel that your creation might be about to come alive, you must then find a lab assistant, some Igor/Ygor/Eyegor fellow ("What hump?") who will look at your work critically and cast his bulging, baleful, doubting eye upon the bloated thing that is your manuscript. Dear would-be author! Feel the fear but reach for lightning! Burn off the dross and dreck of that first draft and ignore the villagers with their traditions and unfounded superstitions, those who lack your vison and imagination and seek to keep you from experimentation and straying from the norm. Torches and pitchforks they may possess, but you, YOU are alive and the characters in your story can breathe and move of their own volition because YOU dare to tamper in God's domain of creation! All of those lofty things - plus you found a good editor, one who gets what you are going for but understands there are certain things that are acceptable and cannot easily be stretched, bent, or ignored. One who will not attempt to alter your authorial voice and make you sound like all the other zombiefied hacks seeking to profit on last year's dead concepts, lying corpse-like at the bottom of Amazon's algorithms.

Don't get spooked, dear writer. The creative power in you is seeking to escape, to burst forth from your chest. But you can control the deep urge by sitting and communing with the spirits who will be embodied within your stories. When that full moon casts its light through the window of your soul and you sense the wolven beast is emerging, chain thyself to the altar of creative flow and purge those demons of doubt, transforming them into servants of story to do your will. By that I mean, sit down, shut off the internet, and write! Write like mad! Wild and crazy, savage and sarcastic, let the bestial nature free to chase and hunt the words and phrases that will give chills of delight to your future readers.

And if during the process of creation, that exploration of narrative flow, you find yourself trapped like Fay Wray in the grip of a giant hairy paw, stuck in the lost world of writer's block, relax a bit and take some notes from your elevated position, whether in the jungles of a tropical island or the jungles of the big city. Consider the fact that someone is giving you a hand. Enjoy the shift in perspective. When you are once again free (and you will be! The biplanes are coming!) give yourself a hand and attack that manuscript with renewed fervor like a Zuni fetish doll in Karen Black's apartment.

And if, after all the mangled metaphors and rack-stretched similes offered above, against all the doom-laden prophesies of the elder gods, you still believe that you are a writer possessed of the talent to craft and weave the stories this world sorely needs, then sharpen your vorpal blade and venture forth, brave soul!

Tell the Tale and Write from the Heart!

Acknowledgements

Writers say that they live in service to their Muse. I agree but must add that the Muse also lives in service to me. It is a partnership and I do the heavy lifting of actually taking her ideas and making them practical. She (yes, I have genderfied my Muse and she is SHE) brings me wild thoughts sometimes, but also solutions to narrative issues small and large.

There are days and nights when she shouts. Other times, when I am paying attention, she whispers. The communication comes in many forms and from many people. Often the initial idea comes out of the blue, as they say. There are a lot of those, and I know it is a good one if it hangs around.

Most of the chapters in this book are brought to you through the Muse tool of Theme. I was given a single word each month and asked to write a blog entry for the OCWriters website. I found it liberating and fun. See if you can guess what the themes were. The answers are listed on the following page. The two people that operate OCWriters.network have a true commitment to assisting writers in honing their craft. They themselves are both skilled authors and work hard at creating worthy tales. It is my great pleasure to be associated with Megan Peticolas Haskell and Greta Boris. If you are writing, you need to be reading their website offerings. Thanks for letting me play in your sandbox, kids!

Regarding my books I am often asked, "Who is your target audience?" My answer invariably is, "Jill." Jill is my partner in everything, and I am very fortunate that she lets me hang out with her. She is my front-line editor, my primary beta reader, and the one who tells me whether I have created something brilliant or if I have misheard my Muse completely. I suspect Jill communicates with my Muse directly when I am not in the room. They drink wine and shake their heads when I get off course. Likely they are shaking their heads right now.

Like most writers I am a reader first. Like some writers I am employed as a content editor. That is a vague term meaning roughly a writer who knows what is working and what is not in someone else's book. This is not something that can be taught. It is often based on opinions formed over the course of a lifetime through voracious reading. It is also formed through conversation with other writers and especially with those marvelous creatures who are more precisely described as line editors. I am blessed to be associated with many.

Writing is often done in the still of the night or the quiet of the morning. Writers get inside their own heads and, when their Muse is upon them, they find it difficult to emerge from the world they are creating. The Muse needs to be fed. Do yourself the great favor of finding a community. I find mine at the Southern California Writers Conference and The Southern California Writers Association. Companions and compatriots, we cheer each other on, learn from one another's mistakes and successes, discuss and dissect the world of publishing and the multitude of changes and alterations. Together we are able to navigate the varied currents of genre, memoir, media, and trends.

I hope you have found this volume helpful. More, I hope you have found it amusing.

THEMES FOR EACH CHAPTER

GOALS - I'd Like to Start Procrastinating

LOVE - Pantsers Become Plotters: A Love Story

GREEN - Searching for Greener Pastures

BEGINNINGS - Crafting Memorable Opening Lines

INSPIRATION - Where Do You Get Your Crazy Ideas?

SUMMER - Writes of Summer

FREEDOM - The Cost of Freedom

HOT - In the Heat of the Moment

BALANCE - Yin and Yang of Storytelling

SCARED - Writing Scared

GRATITUDE - The Grateful Writer

GIFTS - The Gift of the iMagi: Imagination

JEFFREY J. MICHAELS IS A GEMINI. As such he is deeply involved in whatever interests him at the moment.

He describes his short story collection *A Day at the Beach and Other Brief Diversions* as "metaphyictional," combining fantasy and humor with metaphysical elements.

He is currently polishing a sweeping fantasy series of interconnected tales collectively known as The Mystical Histories. It is varied enough that he says he may even finish most of the stories.

Book One of Tasa's Passage Trilogy, *Tasa's Path*, and a short story, *Crossing Jack*, are available on Amazon.

In Jeff's real life he is a well-respected creative and spiritual consultant. He does not like to talk about his award-winning horror story.

*****

For additional inspiring articles from Jeffrey J. Michaels, and information about upcoming events, please visit www.jeffreyjmichaels.com.

www.ingramcontent.com/pod-product-compliance
Lightning Source LLC
Chambersburg PA
CBHW060210070426
42447CB00035B/2934